EARTH'S ENERGY EXPERIMENTS

GEOTHERMAL ENERGY PROJECTS

PROJECTS

Easy Energy Activities for
Future Engineers!

MEGAN BORGERT-SPANIOL

CONSULTING EDITOR, DIANE CRAIG, M.A./READING SPECIALIST

Super Sandcastle

An Imprint of Abdo Publishing
abdopublishing.com

abdopublishing.com

Published by Abdo Publishing, a division of ABDO, PO Box 398166, Minneapolis, Minnesota 55439. Copyright © 2019 by Abdo Consulting Group, Inc. International copyrights reserved in all countries. No part of this book may be reproduced in any form without written permission from the publisher. Super SandCastle™ is a trademark and logo of Abdo Publishing.

Printed in the United States of America, North Mankato, Minnesota
052018
092018

THIS BOOK CONTAINS RECYCLED MATERIALS

Design and Production: Mighty Media, Inc.
Editor: Liz Salzmann
Cover Photographs: Mighty Media, Inc.; Shutterstock
Interior Photographs: Getty Images; iStockphoto; Mighty Media, Inc.; Shutterstock

The following manufacturers/names appearing in this book are trademarks:
Elmer's® Glue-All®, Essential Everyday®, Market Pantry™, Pyrex®, Sharpie®, Smucker's® Magic Shell®

Library of Congress Control Number: 2017961707

Publisher's Cataloging-in-Publication Data
Names: Borgert-Spaniol, Megan, author.
Title: Geothermal energy projects: Easy energy activities for future engineers! / by Megan Borgert-Spaniol.
Other titles: Easy energy activities for future engineers!
Description: Minneapolis, Minnesota : Abdo Publishing, 2019. | Series: Earth's energy experiments
Identifiers: ISBN 9781532115622 (lib.bdg.) | ISBN 9781532156342 (ebook)
Subjects: LCSH: Geothermal resources--Juvenile literature. | Handicraft--Juvenile literature. | Science projects--Juvenile literature. | Earth sciences--Experiments--Juvenile literature.
Classification: DDC 621.44--dc23

Super SandCastle™ books are created by a team of professional educators, reading specialists, and content developers around five essential components—phonemic awareness, phonics, vocabulary, text comprehension, and fluency—to assist young readers as they develop reading skills and strategies and increase their general knowledge. All books are written, reviewed, and leveled for guided reading and early reading intervention programs for use in shared, guided, and independent reading and writing activities to support a balanced approach to literacy instruction.

TO ADULT HELPERS

The projects in this title are fun and simple. There are just a few things to remember to keep kids safe. Some projects require the use of sharp or hot objects. Also, kids may be using messy materials such as glue or paint. Make sure they protect their clothes and work surfaces. Review the projects before starting, and be ready to assist when necessary.

KEY SYMBOLS

Watch for these warning symbols in this book. Here is what they mean.

HOT!
You will be working with something hot. Get help!

SHARP!
You will be working with a sharp object. Get help!

CONTENTS

WHAT IS GEOTHERMAL ENERGY?

Geothermal energy is energy created by Earth's heat. The center of Earth is **extremely** hot. It is hot enough to melt rock! The temperature is cooler closer to Earth's surface. But it is still hot.

MELTED ROCK

This heat warms underground **reservoirs** of water. In some places, this water flows out through cracks in Earth's crust. This creates pools called hot springs. The energy from hot springs can be used for bathing and to heat buildings.

HOT SPRING

People also drill wells deep into Earth's crust to get to the energy. Geothermal energy is a clean energy. It creates little pollution. Geothermal energy is also renewable. It is always being produced by Earth.

However, building geothermal power plants is expensive. And the power often has to be transported long distances to users. Scientists are working on ways to solve these problems.

GEOTHERMAL WELLS

HOW WE USE GEOTHERMAL ENERGY

Geothermal energy has many uses. People can use it directly. They can also use it to heat and cool buildings. Geothermal energy is also used to create electricity.

DIRECT USE

Hot springs are sources of geothermal energy. People have used them for bathing and cooking for thousands of years. Hot springs can be found on all seven continents.

HEATING AND COOLING

Many buildings today have geothermal heat pumps. These pumps draw Earth's heat from underground pipes. This heats the buildings during winter. In warmer months, the pumps draw heat back underground.

ELECTRICITY

Power stations use heat from inside Earth's crust. The heat produces steam. Then, the steam energy is used to **generate** electricity. The United States produces enough geothermal electricity to power more than three million homes!

GEOTHERMAL POWER

There are three main types of geothermal power stations. These are dry steam, flash steam, and binary cycle. All three use the power of steam to turn **turbines**. The turbines help **generate** electricity. Power lines take the electricity to homes and other buildings.

DRY STEAM POWER STATION

A dry steam power station uses natural pockets of underground steam. The steam is directed into a turbine in the power station.

DRY STEAM POWER STATION IN LARDERELLO, ITALY

PIERO GINORI CONTI

Piero Ginori Conti was an Italian businessman. In the early 1900s, Conti explored geothermal power. In 1904, he used natural dry steam to turn a turbine in Larderello, Italy. This powered several light bulbs! In 1911, the world's first geothermal power station was built in Larderello. The station is still active today!

BINARY CYCLE POWER STATION IN CALIFORNIA

FLASH STEAM POWER STATION

A flash steam power station uses hot water from underground. The water is pumped into a tank, where it cools and **evaporates**. This produces steam to power the station's **turbine**.

BINARY CYCLE POWER STATION

A binary cycle power station uses hot water from underground to heat a second liquid. This liquid turns to steam which powers the turbine.

MATERIALS

Here are some of the materials that you will need for the projects in this book.

ALUMINUM CAN

ALUMINUM FOIL

ALUMINUM PIE TIN

BAKING DISH

CHOCOLATE SHELL TOPPING

CINNAMON IMPERIALS CANDIES

CORK

COTTON BALLS

CRAFT GLUE

CRISPY RICE CEREAL

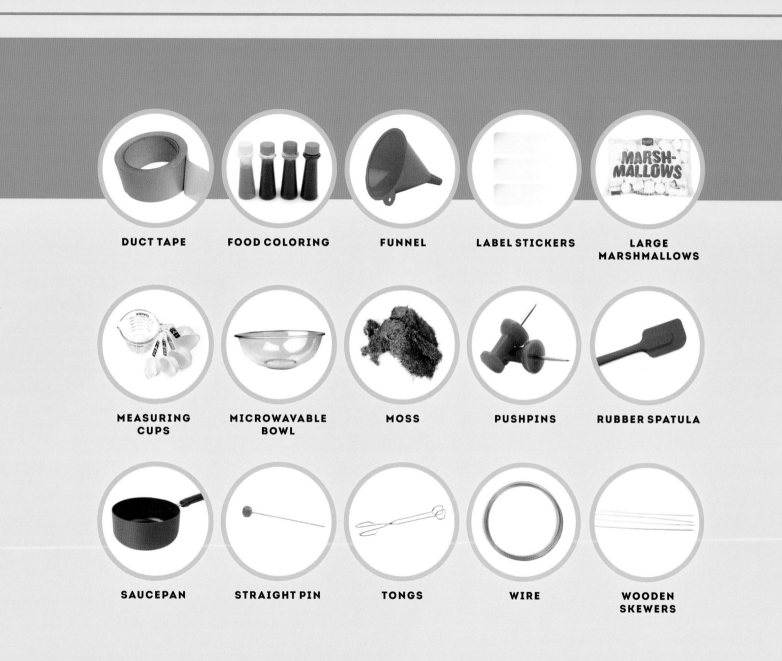

DUCT TAPE

FOOD COLORING

FUNNEL

LABEL STICKERS

LARGE MARSHMALLOWS

MEASURING CUPS

MICROWAVABLE BOWL

MOSS

PUSHPINS

RUBBER SPATULA

SAUCEPAN

STRAIGHT PIN

TONGS

WIRE

WOODEN SKEWERS

LAYERED EARTH TREAT

MATERIALS: microwavable bowl, large marshmallows, butter, microwave oven, rubber spatula, measuring cups, crispy rice cereal, plate, wooden skewer, cinnamon imperials candies, freezer, chocolate shell topping, knife

Earth is made up of layers. The layers closest to Earth's **core** are very hot. The layers get a little cooler closer to the crust. But the crust is still hot enough to provide geothermal energy!

① Place 12 to 14 marshmallows in a bowl. Add 2 tablespoons of butter.

② Heat the bowl in the microwave for 30 seconds.

③ Stir the contents of the bowl.

④ Repeat steps 2 and 3 until the marshmallows are melted.

⑤ Gently stir in 1½ cups of crispy rice cereal.

⑥ Make sure the mixture is cool enough to touch. Wet your hands with water and pull a handful of the mixture from the bowl. Place it on a plate.

⑦ Gently press the mixture flat.

⑧ Use a wooden skewer to poke a hole halfway through a marshmallow.

⑨ Push two cinnamon imperials into the hole in the marshmallow.

Continued on the next page.

10 Place the marshmallow on the flattened cereal mixture.

11 Fold the cereal mixture around the marshmallow. Add more cereal mixture to fill in any gaps.

12 Press the layers together to form a firm ball.

13 Put the ball in the freezer for about 10 minutes.

14 Remove the ball from the freezer. Coat the ball with chocolate shell topping. Make sure the whole ball is covered.

15 Put the ball back in the freezer for about 10 minutes. This is your model of Earth!

16 Have an adult help you cut the Earth model in half. Observe the four layers. The cinnamon imperials and marshmallow are the **inner** and **outer cores**. The cereal mixture is the mantle, and the chocolate shell is the crust!

Earth's layers are the **inner** and **outer cores**, mantle, and crust.

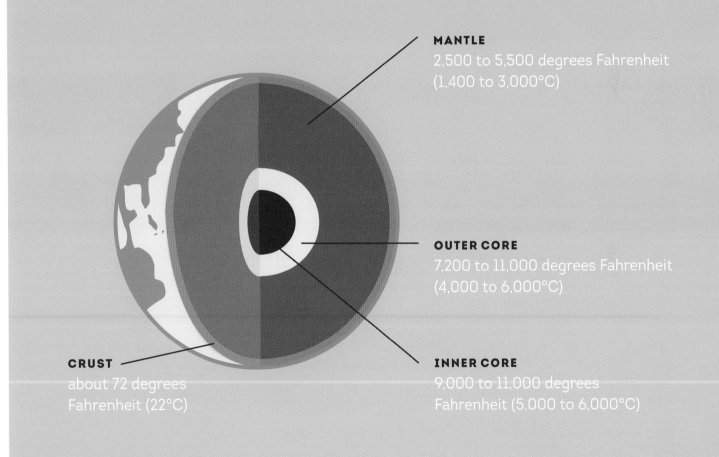

MANTLE
2,500 to 5,500 degrees Fahrenheit
(1,400 to 3,000°C)

OUTER CORE
7,200 to 11,000 degrees Fahrenheit
(4,000 to 6,000°C)

CRUST
about 72 degrees
Fahrenheit (22°C)

INNER CORE
9,000 to 11,000 degrees
Fahrenheit (5,000 to 6,000°C)

KINETIC ENERGY IN JARS

MATERIALS: narrow baking dish, water, 2 label stickers, markers, 2 clear jars, ice cubes, tongs, food coloring, wooden skewer

Underground pockets of water are warmed by Earth's heat. The heat increases the motion of **molecules** in the water. As water gets hotter, its molecules move faster. This **kinetic energy** is what turns water into steam. It is also the reason why hot water rises above cold water!

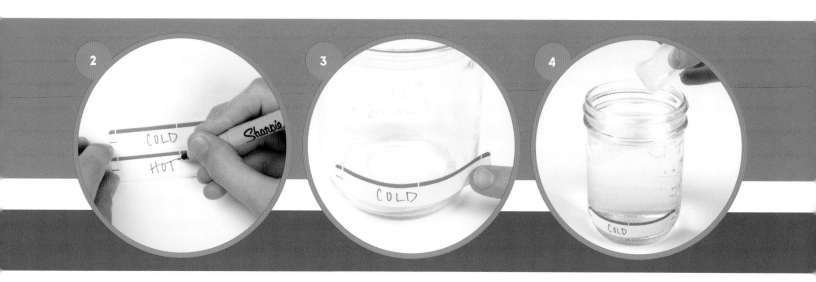

1. Fill the baking dish one-third full with water. Set it aside to let the water become room temperature.

2. Write "COLD" on one label. Write "HOT" on the other label.

3. Stick a label to each jar.

4. Fill the jar marked "COLD" with cold tap water. Add a few ice cubes to make the water colder.

5. Fill the jar marked "HOT" with hot tap water.

Continued on the next page.

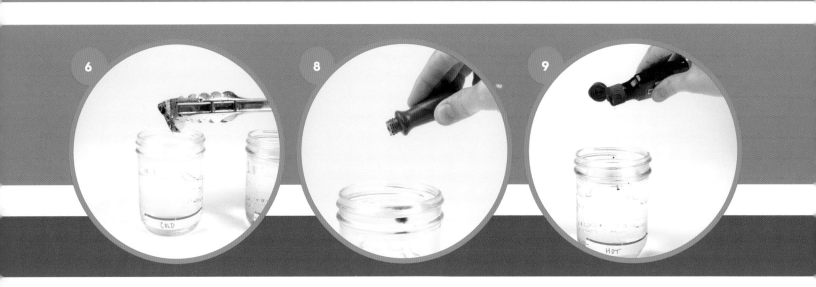

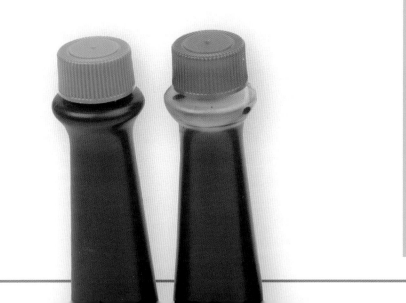

6 Remove the ice cubes from the jar with cold water.

8 Add a drop of blue food coloring to the cold water.

9 Add a drop of red food coloring to the hot water.

7 Place the jars next to each other.

10 Observe how the color moves in each type of water. How does the water temperature affect the movement of the food coloring?

11 Stir the water in each jar.

12 Set the baking dish of water between the jars. Hold one of the jars in each hand.

13 Carefully pour the cold and hot water into opposite ends of the baking dish at the same time.

14 Observe how the cold and hot water mix with the water in the baking dish. After a few minutes, the hot water should rise to the top of the dish.

FUNNEL GEYSER

MATERIALS: saucepan, water, funnel, aluminum foil, stove

Geothermal heat can escape from underground through geysers. Geysers are hot springs that sometimes erupt with water or steam. Countries such as Iceland and New Zealand use geysers to heat swimming pools, greenhouses, and more.

① Fill a saucepan three-fourths full of water.

② Place the funnel upside down in the saucepan. The stem of the funnel should stick out of the water.

③ Tear off a piece of aluminum foil a little bigger than the saucepan. Make a hole in the center of the foil.

④ Place the foil over the pan with the funnel sticking through the hole.

⑤ Wrap the foil tightly around the edges of the saucepan. Be sure the foil doesn't reach the bottom of the pan.

⑥ Repeat steps 3 through 5 to add a second layer of foil.

⑦ Wrap a strip of foil around the base of the funnel to seal any cracks.

⑧ Place the saucepan on the stove. Set the burner to high.

⑨ Wait for the water to boil. Then watch your geyser erupt!

⑩ Turn the stove off.

FUMAROLE LANDSCAPE

MATERIALS: aluminum pie tin, pushpin, nail, newspaper, paint, paintbrush, craft glue, sand, rocks, moss, cotton balls, saucepan about as wide as the pie tin, water, aluminum foil, stove

Geothermal heat can also escape through fumaroles. These are vents in Earth's surface that **emit** steam and hot gases. They are often found near **volcanoes**. In California, one of the world's largest geothermal power stations uses steam from fumaroles.

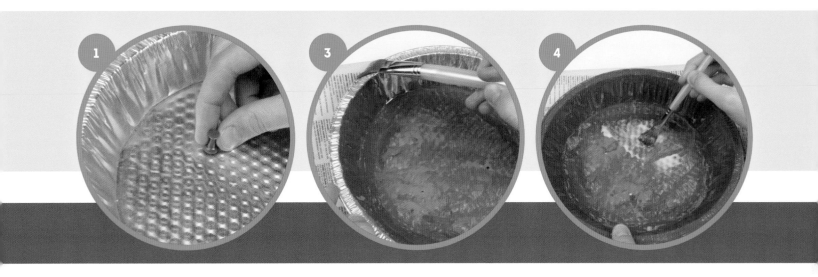

1. Use a pushpin to poke two to four holes in the bottom of the pie tin. The holes can be wherever you choose.

2. Push a nail through the holes to make them a little bigger.

3. Cover your work surface with newspaper. Paint the inside of the tin so it looks like a rocky **landscape**. Use colors such as brown, gray, orange, red, and green. Don't paint over the holes. Let the paint dry.

4. Brush an uneven layer of glue over the surface of the pie tin. Do not brush glue over the holes.

Continued on the next page.

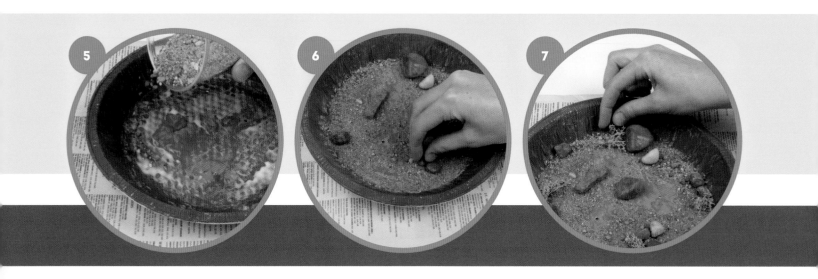

5 Sprinkle coarse sand over the glue. Turn the pie tin over to pour out any extra sand.

6 Place rocks on the sand in the pie tin.

7 Place bits of moss around the pie tin **landscape**.

8 Pull a cotton ball into small pieces. Stretch the cotton pieces until you can see through them.

9 Add the cotton pieces to the pie tin **landscape**. These represent rising steam.

10 Fill the saucepan halfway with water.

11 Cover the saucepan with two layers of aluminum foil. Wrap the foil tightly around the edges of the saucepan. Be sure the foil doesn't reach the bottom of the pan.

12 Place the pie tin on top of the saucepan. Carefully push the nail through the holes in the pie tin to make holes in the foil.

13 Place the saucepan on the stove. Set the burner to high. Wait for the water to boil. Then watch as steam comes out through your fumaroles!

14 Turn the stove off.

TIN CAN POWER STATION

MATERIALS: empty aluminum can, hammer, nail, aluminum pie tin, marker, scissors, ruler, straight pin, sturdy wire, duct tape, cork, saucepan, water, aluminum foil, stove

The dry steam power station is the simplest kind of geothermal power station. It funnels steam from underground directly into **turbines**. The steam hits the blades of the turbine, causing the turbine to spin. A **generator** uses this motion to create electricity!

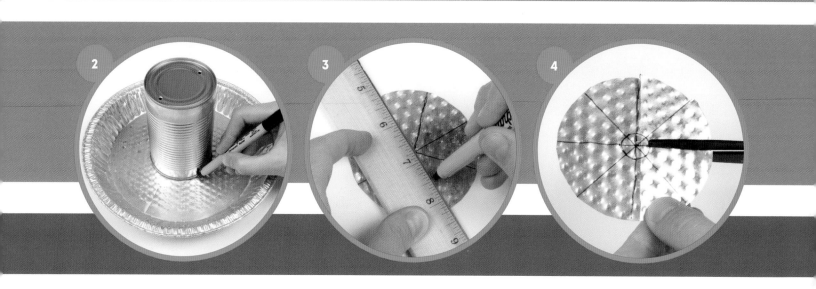

1. Have an adult help you use a hammer and nail to make two holes in the bottom of the can. The holes should be opposite each other near the edge.

2. Set the can in the center of the pie tin. Trace around the can. Cut out the circle.

3. Use a ruler and marker to divide the circle into eight equal sections. Draw a circle around the point where all the sections meet. The circle should be ½ inch (0.6 cm) across.

4. Cut along each line. Stop cutting when you reach the small circle.

Continued on the next page.

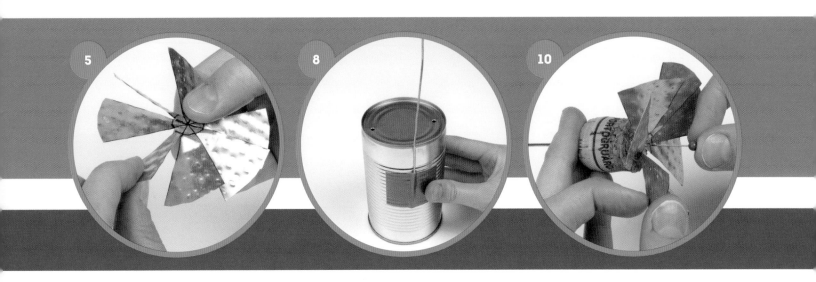

5 Now you should have eight separate sections connected in the middle. These are the blades of the **turbine**. Twist each blade slightly. Be sure to twist them in the same direction.

6 Poke a straight pin through the center of the turbine. Wiggle the pin to enlarge the hole slightly.

7 Place the can with the bottom facing up. Cut a piece of sturdy wire that is twice as long as the height of the can.

8 Hold the wire against the outside of the can so one end sticks straight up. Duct tape the other end to the middle of the can.

9 Push the free end of the wire into the cork.

10 Push the turbine's pin into the side of the cork opposite from the wire.

11 Bend the wire so the **turbine** hangs about 2 inches (5 cm) above the can.

12 Fill a saucepan halfway with water. Cover the saucepan with two layers of aluminum foil. Wrap the foil tightly around the edges of the saucepan. Be sure the foil doesn't reach the bottom of the pan.

13 Use a nail to gently poke a hole through the center of both layers of foil.

14 Place the saucepan on the stove. Set the burner to high.

15 Wait for the water to boil. When steam comes out of the hole in the foil, place the aluminum can over the hole.

16 Observe the turbine. Within a minute, steam coming out of the can's holes will turn the turbine! If the turbine does not spin, try making the hole in the foil bigger. Moving the turbine farther away from the top of the can may help too.

17 Turn the stove off.

CONCLUSION

Geothermal energy is energy created by Earth's heat. This energy escapes through Earth's crust. People use the energy for heating and electricity. Geothermal energy is renewable. It is always being produced inside Earth!

QUIZ

1. What is the heat in the center of Earth hot enough to do?

2. Hot springs are found on all seven continents.
   TRUE OR FALSE?

3. Where was the world's first geothermal power station built?

LEARN MORE ABOUT IT!

You can find out more about geothermal energy at the library. Or you can ask an adult to help you **research** geothermal energy on the internet!

Answers: 1. Melt rock 2. True 3. Larderello, Italy

GLOSSARY

core – the center of a space object such as a planet, moon, or star.

emit – to send out.

evaporate – to change from a liquid into a gas.

extremely – very great in degree or severity.

generate – to create or produce.

generator – a machine that creates electricity.

inner – on the inside.

kinetic energy – energy associated with motion.

landscape – an area of land that has a particular quality or appearance.

molecule – a group of two or more atoms that make up the smallest piece of a substance.

outer – on the outside.

research – to find out more about something.

reservoir – a place where something is stored.

turbine – a machine that produces power when it is rotated at high speed.

volcano – a deep opening in Earth's surface from which hot liquid rock or steam comes out.